THE VESTRYMAN'S MANUAL

THE VESTRYMAN'S MANUAL

BY HOWARD HARPER

THE SEABURY PRESS • NEW YORK

Fourth Printing 1969

Copyright © 1964 by The Seabury Press, Incorporated
Library of Congress Catalog Card Number: 64-12940
Design by Nancy H. Dale
453-369-Hm-17.5-5
Printed in the United States of America

ACKNOWLEDGMENTS

KIPLING said of Homer that "wot 'e thought 'e might require, 'e went and took" and adds, as if the ancient plagiarist had set an acceptable precedent, "the same as me."

In this book I join the company of Homer and Kipling. I went and took quotations from the sermon "The True Function of a Parish" by the Rev. John Heuss, which appear in Chapter IV. From the Rev. Robert N. Rodenmayer's *The Pastor's Prayerbook* (New York: Oxford University Press, 1960), I lifted prayers for the service of installation of a Vestryman.

I drew on the wisdom and experience of National Council officers for material that would otherwise not have occurred to me, and I put myself forever in the debt of Mr. John Sherwood, of Southern Ohio, who made available the results of his two-year Vestry Study.

I am indebted to Mr. John W. Reinhardt for his penetrating thoughts on stewardship which are reflected throughout Chapter 10.

Also I leaned heavily on the encyclopedic knowledge of the Rev. Canon Charles Guilbert, who patiently explained several of the Canons whenever it was necessary, and there were quite a few such times. Canon Guilbert also contributed the two

5

services in the Appendix, which are adaptations from *The Book of Offices* (New York: The Church Pension Fund, 1960).

For all the help they gave me, both unknowingly and by design, I am grateful to these good friends.

CONTENTS

1 WHY A MANUAL
FOR VESTRYMEN?

HARDLY ANYONE believes the Canons really mean what they say about Vestrymen. That is the reason for this book. The national Canon is clear: "the Vestry shall be agents and legal representatives of the Parish in all matters concerning its corporate property and the relations of the Parish to its Clergy." Generally speaking, the diocesan Canons say pretty much the same thing. That would seem to be all anyone had to know.

But there is commanding evidence that many of today's Vestrymen are by no means inclined to settle for this. If they were, they would attend to the business affairs of the parish to the best of their ability and on occasion try to smooth over those little clergy-laity tiffs that nibble at the unity of parish life—and that would be that.

Instead, they write innumerable letters appealing for help. In recent years they have been writing thousands of such letters to publishers, to Executive Council departments, and to thoughtful individuals whom they consider qualified to guide them. They want, they say, a handbook or a manual for Vestrymen.

Just what sort of handbook is the Vestryman looking for? Certainly not a set of instructions on how to be a good businessman. Either he is one or he isn't, and there is not much a book can do about it one way or the other. And certainly he is not asking for a course on how to be a mediator between clergy and people. There are no gimmicks in the art of peacemaking; besides, not all relations between people and clergy are belligerent ones.

What he is looking for is a larger treatment of his job than the one given in the Canons' minimal statements, because he already has a larger picture in his mind. He knows that the layman has emerged from his traditional passive role as spectator in a clergyman's Church and is finding his place as a full-time participant in the Church's total ministry to the world. As a Vestryman, therefore, he is increasingly aware that he was not elected just to pay bills and worry about personality clashes. He hopes to be a leader in the deepening life of his parish and its growing ministry to the world around it.

But he knows that a leader must have information, knowledge, training, and vision. And he feels that he needs help in acquiring these assets.

That is the kind of help this book aims to give him.

2 SOME HISTORY

A VESTRY is really a room near the altar where the vestments are kept. Our application of the word to a group of parish officers comes from the fact that in its formative days the group used to hold its meetings in this room.

Vestries as we know them are rather peculiarly an American institution. We get the term, but that's about all, from the Church of England. The English Church has Wardens and Vestrymen, but their rights and duties furnish no pattern for ours, partly because the Church of England is a State Church, and partly because our Vestry Canon was not crystallized until 1904, a century and a quarter after we became independent of, and had largely forgotten our ties with, England.

The early Church had no Vestry of any kind. Organization was not needed in those days. By the time the Church had grown to the point where it did have property to look after and an income to spend, the clergy took control and the laity had no say in these matters.

Late in the Middle Ages the first Churchwarden appears. His job was to keep the nave in repair. Note that he stayed out of the chancel and sanctuary. These holy places were off limits to a layman.

Also in those days there began to be the lay office of sidesmen (really synodsmen, but you know how the British telescope their words), whose duty it was to report to the Bishop at synods telling him, under oath, just what was the moral condition of the parishes from which they came.

By the time of the American colonization the Church here had Wardens and Vestrymen, still of course within the limitations of the Established, or State, Church of which it was a part. After the American Revolution, when the Church here was independent of both the English and the American governments, there was a great deal of confusion, and indeed some real battles over the status of the Vestry.

The Vestry's rights, relations, and duties needed redefinition, but it was terribly slow in coming. Not until the General Convention of 1877 did the Church face the problem. This General Convention appointed a joint commission "to consider and report to the next General Convention what are the several functions of Rector, Wardens, and Vestrymen in the control and administration of the parishes."

The problem proved too much for the commission to solve in three years. They were told in 1880 to keep at it, but by 1883 they still had no answer and were instructed to try again. The present Canon 13 was not achieved until 1904. In the meantime, confusion continued in varying degrees in the various dioceses. But the mills of the Church grind slowly.

All we can say we inherited from the Church of England is the idea of a board of laymen, plus the terms "Warden" and "Vestryman." It is interesting to note that in general practice we have dropped the English terms "Rector's Warden" and "People's Warden" and replaced them with the "Senior" and "Junior" terminology of the Masonic Lodge. Note also that in the Canons they are simply called Wardens. The words Junior and Senior are not used at all.

One of the most notable trends in current Church history is

the growing practice of granting women eligibility to serve on Vestries. The recognition of women's place in the general life of the community was officially declared in 1920 when the Nineteenth Amendment was ratified. Vast cultural changes have resulted.

But the Church, always conservative, has not yet adopted its Nineteenth Amendment. Women are not yet given full status in the life of the Church, and it may be some little while before the Church catches up with the times.

> Our fathers have been Churchmen
> Nineteen hundred years or so,
> And to every new suggestion
> They have always answered No!

Nevertheless, it can only be a matter of time. The movement toward admitting that women are people is irresistible.

In 1946, Mrs. Randolph H. Dyer of Missouri, having been elected a deputy to General Convention, appeared at Philadelphia and took her lone seat in an otherwise unanimously male House of Deputies without, as far as the record shows, any fuss. But when at the 1949 General Convention three women showed up with full credentials, panic struck. One woman had not been enough to frighten six hundred men; three amounted to a portent and a threat. By a vote of 321 to 242 the men declined to accept them as Deputies. The men did, however, offer to seat them without voice or vote, to which the ladies said a firm "No, thank you."

One result of the disturbance was the appointment, at this same General Convention, of a joint commission (three Bishops, three clergymen, three laymen, and three women) "to consider the problem [sic] of giving the women a voice in the legislation of General Convention." In 1952 the joint commission reported that the problem could be solved very easily by changing the word "Laymen" to "Lay Deputies" and "Layman" to "Lay Deputy" where these words appear in the Constitution.

No action was taken on the commission's report, but its simple suggestion about the change of a word furnished the basis for resolutions in 1955 and 1958, which were lost, and for another in 1961, which was referred to a joint committee to be reported on in 1964.

Thus does the machinery sputter and groan. The Church is in no hurry. And while the dawdling goes on, the girls may continue their ecclesiastical KP duties, their powerful financial support of the Church's mission, and their chores, but the boys are going to run the Church.

In the dioceses and the parishes the outlook is brighter. Nearly 60 per cent of our dioceses now make no distinction between men and women in their conventions, and the number of these increases yearly. Ordinarily this automatically means also that women are eligible to serve on Vestries. It is difficult to believe that this growing majority will not ultimately vote to do in General Convention what they are already doing in diocese and parish.

That human nature is a strange phenomenon is no news to anyone. Human inconsistency, not surprisingly, shows up in this matter of desegregating women, just as it does everywhere else in life. Even in those parishes that are perfectly free to put women on their Vestries, less than one out of twelve Vestry members are women. There is a lag between our intellectual convictions and our emotionally colored habits of action. Apparently our attitude is that women ought to be eligible, but that doesn't mean we are going to vote for them.

Old patterns die slowly, but they do die. The women of the Church can count on recognition some day, frustrating though the interim period may be.

Because of their guaranteed future, women are not dealt

with separately as women in this book. Looking ahead, we treat them herein as full-fledged members of the Church. All terms used—Vestryman, parishioner, etc.—are intended to mean either men or women.

The world changes and life changes with it. The Church adjusts, however slowly, to new needs and new approaches to its ministry. The structure of the parish (including, of course, the Vestry) goes along with the evolution of corporate life in the world we are here to serve.

Our Vestry system was conceived and solidified in a culture that was basically agrarian, with each community standing as an almost self-sufficient unit. Since those days we have by imperceptible steps become an urban culture. Undeniably, even though your parish is in a village in the middle of the corn belt, you are now part of a milieu in which the cast of thought is much the same as it would be if you lived in New York, Dallas, or Seattle. Like it or not, we all think as only city people used to think. We have our morning papers, our national TV programs, our mobility of population, our social security numbers, our credit cards, and all the other depersonalizing factors that weaken local individuality and bring us all into a nearly uniform total state of mind. This does not mean we are brain washed. It means rather that we are all in the same sociological boat.

What it implies about the future function of the Vestry remains to be seen, and cannot be predicted in this book. There are those today who are talking about abolishing the parish system and meeting present needs through specialized ministries, dealing with special and perhaps transitory issues. Seminary faculties, of all denominations, say that so many of their students are preparing for specialties—college, industry, armed forces, the aging, etc.—that they worry about the impending short supply of parish clergy. It does not now appear likely, however, that such an extreme situation will continue indefinitely.

But, facing the loss of community in our lives and the divisions of people into categories—race, labor, suburban, aging, liberal, conservative, inner city, youth, and so on—it will certainly be necessary for the parish either to find ways of ministering to these groups separately or of bringing them back into an uncategorized unity. In the light of our Christian hope that the human family may achieve unity while preserving all its diverse identities, one would assume that the latter would be our goal. In either case, there are implications for the Vestryman which cannot at this point be foreseen.

Here in this book we must work with what is permanent: the Vestryman's knowledge of the true nature of the Church and his relationship with Rector, people, diocese, and Executive Council. Whatever happens, short of the complete breakdown of the parish system, these are not likely to undergo radical change. And if we thought the parish (and Vestry) were in danger of being abolished, there would be no point in writing this book at all.

3 YOUR QUALIFICATIONS

IF YOU have just become a Vestryman and are doing a bit of worrying right now, you are perfectly normal. Any new Vestryman worth his salt goes through the stage of wondering why the parish elected him and how he is going to do the kind of job he hopes to do.

It isn't the legal qualifications and duties laid down by the Canons that are frightening. They are, as a matter of fact, rather dull. The new Vestryman is troubled by those aspects of his position that are new and beyond the Canons—the aspects that have to do with ministry, not routine.

What a man wants to know is, "Am I the right person to take leadership in the ministry of this parish, and how do I learn the job?"

Don't waste time telling yourself the parish must have made a mistake in electing you. In every Church job, from sexton to Presiding Bishop, the Lord has to make do with what he gets. If he waited for the perfect person every time, there would be quite a few vacancies in Church positions. He can use you with all your limitations.

No, your problem is how, with the native equipment you have, you can *become* a good Vestryman. For that question there are specific, detailed answers. Let's skip the preaching and assume you already know God did not commission your parish to nourish itself into social and financial success, but rather to become an instrument for his use—both among your members and in the community around you.

Let's go on from there and talk about the things you will have to know in order to be both a leader in your parish's life and ministry and a competent guardian of the solvency it has to have in order not to be distracted from its primary job.

Here is an outline of what you will need to know and understand.

The relationship between you (and, of course, the other Vestrymen) and your Rector.

The relationship between you (and, again, the other Vestrymen) and the people who have selected you as one who can speak both for them and to them.

The relationship between your parish and your diocese.

The relationship between your parish and the National Council.

How your Vestry could be organized to involve maximum participation by the people of the parish.

How to achieve fiscal control in parish business affairs.

And, of course, as a theme running through it all, the nature and purpose of the Church. *What is your parish in business for?* All your important decisions will be colored by the way you feel about this question.

Things like these are about all a book can tell you—informational things. It can't give you judgment or common sense or depth of faith. Let's not worry about that either. The fact that your friends and neighbors elected you must mean they think you already have a good start on those qualities.

Your training—well, that's something else. Whatever your qualifications, you *will* need training. We will go into that in the next section.

4 YOU AND THE RECTOR

THE FIRST FACT to be considered is that your Rector is a *member* of the Vestry. Unless state law specifies otherwise, the Vestry consists of "Rector, Wardens, and Vestrymen." You and he are not in any kind of competition. You and the Rector are partners in the administrative matters of the parish and, inevitably, in setting the tone of parish life generally.

When there is friction between Rector and Vestry, surveys (and experience) show it is likely to be in the area of business affairs that they arise. The usual attitude, too familiar to need discussion here, is that the average clergyman doesn't know anything about business. And if you mean production, sales, service, and profits, it is probably true that his knowledge is meager.

But that is not the kind of business the Church is in, and you would do well to consider that your sound business sense and the Rector's concentration on the quality of parish life may together form the happy fusion of viewpoints that will bring about a right handling of your affairs.

Admittedly, there are many more illustrations than we need to show how frequently clergymen do seem allergic to sensible finance—like the Rector who went out on his own and bought one hundred $2 hymnals at half-price and boasted that he had "saved" the parish $100. This sort of thing exasperates Vestry-men, and rightly. Vestry and Rector must have it firmly under-stood that neither the Rector nor anyone else spends money without authorization. Proper fiscal control will head off many heated recriminations.

It is also admittedly true that Vestries are sometimes more concerned about controlling money than about spending it constructively. It is a habit of the businessman's mind to want to see a balance in the bank. You are in your own business to make money. It is almost instinctive with you to think about parish business in the same terms.

But the Church is not in business to make money. There is an important difference between the Rector's point of view and yours about this. People give their money to the Church so that the Church's work may be done. They do not give it to build up a balance; they give it to be spent. With proper allow-ances for items like property maintenance, which must be protected against emergencies, your parish should have a zero balance on December 31. This is how your Rector sees it. It requires a union of your habits of thought and his to get your money matters in their true perspective. With a clear under-standing and acceptance on both sides of the contribution each concept of Church finance can make, you and the Rector can go on to the important part of your relationship.

It is difficult to find a satisfactory analogy to illustrate the relation between Rector and Vestry. If we take as an example the great American game of baseball, we could say the people are the players, the Vestrymen are the coaches, and the Rector is the manager. That is fairly close but it won't quite do, be-cause the Vestrymen and the Rector are players, too. They don't just stand by and tell others how to play.

To say the Rector is the President and the Vestrymen are his Cabinet may help a little, but does not quite fit, either.

But such descriptions do give a little light. They say at least that you are in a special intermediary position between the leader and those he leads. In the Rector's task of molding your parish into a ministering body, you Vestrymen are his assistants, his planning board, his board of strategy, and his executive staff.

When you get into this area of your partnership, the Rector is the specialist. He has training and a knowledge of resources that no one else in the parish has. He is a professional and you are an amateur. Also, he knows the parish as a whole better than anyone else, because from where he sits he sees it as a whole and because he is able to give his full time to knowing it.

So, in this part of your relationship you are in territory where his guidance or his analysis is of fundamental importance. This is by no means to say that you have no initiative in the planning of parish programs and projects. You are not a rubber stamp. If you have ideas of your own, share them. But it does mean that when the Rector puts his finger on a weak spot or proposes an idea the chances are he knows what he is talking about, and it is your job to get with it and help to plan and carry out some constructive action.

Here, as we shall in almost every other section of this book, we come up against the Vestryman's personal need for the deepest possible understanding of the true function of the Church. Only as your sights are set on the right target will you think and plan and work along the right lines with your Rector.

We are all indebted to the Rev. John Heuss for a concise statement of the function of a parish. He enumerates five characteristics a Christian parish must have. In paraphrase, they are as follows:

1. A parish is to be a fellowship of people who have had a soul-shaking personal experience with Jesus Christ.

2. A parish puts its genuine trust in God and does not worry much about its own self-preservation.

3. It is a Spirit-filled community whose whole purpose is to let the world know the good news of salvation through God.

4. It has a glad awareness of the forgiveness of sin.

5. It cares little for any organization except such as is necessary for worship, teaching, and the care of the needy.

To acquire these five basic qualities is the true function of a parish.

Just in case this sounds like a pious ideal, let's ask how "meeting the Lord" or "having a personal experience of Jesus Christ" would be expressed in the layman's normal vocabulary.

All right, put it this way. It means to be socked right in the middle of where you live by the realization that Jesus is a living person whom you can know and relate to just as you can to any other person. The only difference is that he is perfect and you—well, you know what you are. That's what makes this realization a shattering thing: to think that Jesus Christ wants a personal relationship with you, *as you are*.

Once this hits you, it upsets everything. The Lord said it is like being born again, starting a new life with a fresh outlook. It is much more comfortable to go on thinking of Jesus as a long-dead teacher whose teachings we should try to live up to. A sarcastic parody on John 3:16 says: "God so loved the world that two thousand years ago he inspired a certain Jew to say something in favor of good conduct." Really, we all like it that way. It makes us comfortable to think of Christianity as just trying to live a good life.

But that's not it. That "certain Jew" is still living, and he can be involved in your life. And that can be most uncomfortable. They did not crucify Jesus for exhorting people to try to be good.

In spite of our intellectual difficulties with this idea, we really do believe it, you know. Wordsworth said, "Milton!

Thou shouldst be living at this hour. England hath need of thee." Can you imagine yourself saying "Jesus! Thou shouldst be living at this hour. Our parish hath need of thee"? Instinctively we know there is something wrong with that.

We *do* feel that he is living, even though we are terribly inarticulate about it. To meet him personally and have your life totally refocused by that personal association is the goal of your Vestry training.

You as a Vestryman are involved with your Rector in the development of a parish filled with people who know Jesus personally. Once you have this view of your job, your Vestry meetings and your relationship with the Rector will take on meaning, urgency, directness, and vitality.

How do you become that kind of Vestryman, equipped to work intelligently toward that kind of parish? Let's talk a little about Vestry training.

Training: The training of Vestrymen should be the first thing you and your Rector plan together. You will have to agree at the outset that it cannot be done by setting a little time aside at the monthly Vestry meetings. Your term of office would be over before you were half trained for your job. You will have to figure on setting aside a week end or two, and you probably will want to get away somewhere together.

As you and the Rector work on your plans for Vestry training, there is one big point to keep in mind at all times. You are not planning a how-to-do-it course. Look again at Dr. Heuss's five points. They all have to do with a spirit, a climate of the soul; they do not have to do with a course of intellectual subject matter. The purpose of your training is not to give you a list of answers but to give you an experience out of which you will produce the creative answer to the problems that come before you, as they come.

You want to know, in your heart as well as in your mind: what it is to meet the Lord? what it is to belong to a fellowship of men and women who have met him? what it is to have your guilt lifted by an awareness of God's forgiveness?

These are personal experiences, not technical information. They will come to you best in a Retreat, not in a course. And they will need to be continually nourished in occasional Quiet Days. Please think about it this way as you plan your Vestry training.

Having once had even a glimpse of these experiences, you will begin to know with an inner knowledge what God wants your parish to be. You will begin to put organization and money out of the center of parish life and into the supportive position where they belong.

Your concerns will change. Your Vestry will see that its task is to help bring these same experiences into the lives of the people in the parish, and your test of your agenda and your action will be: to what extent do they forward our true purpose?

Then to the degree that your parish becomes a fellowship of forgiven people who have met the Lord, there will arise new questions of your relationship with the world around you. And to all proposals for action in the community you will apply the same test: will this help the people involved to know our Lord as we know him?

Before all else, training for service as a Vestryman is toward the attainment of this sensitive standard of judgment. Your training is a matter of getting your antenna set to a new wave length.

5 YOU AND
THE PARISHIONERS

THE CANON SAYS you are an agent and legal representative "of the Parish in all matters concerning . . . the relations of the Parish with its Clergy." Clearly, the people are your constituency. You are *their* agent and representative.

It is a commentary on our parish life in general that we almost automatically tend to draw a negative inference here. We assume it means "the relations of the parish *versus* its clergy." Why? What makes us take for granted that the purpose of this simple canonical statement is to set you up as a referee or as counsel for the plaintiff?

There is a very good reason why, and we had better deal with it before we try to talk about the positive side of your relations with the people. The reason is that for many, many years we have gone along with a false idea of the nature and purpose of the Church.

This is not an exaggeration. We have thought of the parish as consisting of a group of patrons who have hired an ordained man to minister to them. To the extent that this attitude prevails in your parish, you as the representative of these patrons will be on the receiving end of all the old familiar complaints:

the Rector doesn't make enough calls; he preaches too long; he neglects the parish for community affairs; he mixes religion and politics; I don't agree with what he says; and so on and on and on. All of which means he does not please us paying customers. He does not serve this ecclesiastical club of ours as an employee should.

Rest assured that your job is no such silly business as trying to make several hundred bosses happy with the performance of an employee. Your relations with the people are basically creative, not conciliatory.

This is where it becomes necessary that you yourself have a sound knowledge of the nature and purpose of the Church. When *you* see the parish as a ministering family with the Rector as the leader and teacher in its ministry, then you will begin, sometimes without even knowing it, to help the people change their concept. Your real task here is to make them see themselves as members of an outward-looking group, serving instead of being served. They and you and the Rector are God's team in your area. The Rector is not there to please or entertain or put his parishioners at ease. He is there to direct, strengthen, and nourish them as they try to do what God created your parish to do.

Archbishop Temple once said, "The Church is the only society whose chief purpose is to serve those who for the most part are not her members."

As a Vestryman, you have a special responsibility in helping the people to understand themselves as such a society. How to do it? One answer is that, if this idea is real to you, there will be a contagion that can't fail to make it real—to at least some of your people.

Of course there is more to it than that. You can't leave it all up to the hope that some of your attitude about the Church will rub off, though certainly a great deal will.

There are various studies to which we can look for definite statements parishioners themselves have made in reply to questions about how they want to be related to the Vestrymen.

They say they want you to be available for consultation. They don't want you to be too busy to see them when they need to see you. They go beyond mere availability, however. Many of them use the word "rapport." They want more than a listening post; they want a response, an empathy, and an exchange.

Parishioners want you to be a leader. They don't say what they want to be led in or led to. They are talking about a quality they want you to have. Of course, leadership is not something you can turn on and off. Either you have it or you don't. But the fact that you have been elected to the Vestry must mean that you have some of it. Your inside familiarity with the purpose and program of the parish will open up in your own mind certain areas in which you can help people to find their directions.

Parishioners want, for some mysterious psychological reason, to set you apart as an example to the rank and file of parish membership. This is probably frightening. You know you are no better than they are. It is not fair that they should expect you to be. They should take you as you are, as God does. The best you can do on this is just to do the best you can. Attend services regularly, do your job as you see it, and don't bog down in guilt because you are a sinner like everyone else.

The Rector hopes you will be a two-way communicator, using whatever opportunities you have to keep the people informed about the parish program, and keeping him informed about what is on the people's minds.

In answer to a questionnaire sent to thousands of Vestrymen by the staff of *The Episcopalian*, the Vestrymen appeared to say that aside from the usual money and leadership difficulties two of their greatest problems with the parishioners were: squabbles among the people, and apathy. These would seem to represent two extremes. Certainly the squabblers are not apathetic, and the apathetic ones do not squabble.

No one can make a blueprint for your handling of all these problems in your relationships with the parishioners. You are a communicator, a consultant, a peacemaker, and a reporter. You don't know when you are going to be called upon to be any or all of these, or when your opportunities will appear, or what the nature of an opportunity will be when it does appear. We all like the security of having detailed how-to-do-it instructions for our jobs. But these are areas of life in which we cannot get charts and check lists. There is not that much formulation in life itself. You play it by ear all the way. You will fail often, but there will be many times when you will succeed when you think you have failed.

6 YOU AND THE DIOCESE

WE ANNOUNCE to the world that we are an *Episcopal* Church. What this means literally is that we are a church that has Bishops. It does not set us apart from the rest of Christendom. Rome has Bishops; Orthodoxy has Bishops; Methodism has them, though Methodist Bishops are not quite the same kind. What it all means is that, along with other Communions, we think of the Church as being larger than our local parish. You are not just a member of St. Somebody's parish. Your parish is also a part of a geographical unit known as a diocese and headed by a Bishop. (How much further your membership goes we will discuss in the next chapter.)

This sounds fine in theory. The trouble is that studies show (and we wouldn't need studies to tell us this) that the state of mind of Episcopalians, Vestrymen included, is almost completely "congregationalist." Bishop and diocese are remote to us. We think of the diocese as "they," not "we." The Bishop comes to confirm a class once or twice a year, and we roll out the carpet for him, but beyond his function as a confirming machine we have little notion of who he is or what he does. People from the diocese, particularly the promotion department, come around from time to time and ask us for money, and we try to be as amiable (and as economical) as we can about these invasions. But what they do with the money we feel "we" ought to give "them" is pretty vague to us. We are sure we could have spent it better in our own parish, where we know good causes that are suffering for lack of support.

Let's face the fact that we are more inclined to be Congregationalists than Episcopalians.

But let's also look at why the Lord needs a Bishop and a diocese.

In the first place, we are committed to a Lord who wants his love, and forgiveness, and judgment known *everywhere*, not only in places where there are enough people to finance a parish. Your Bishop has been given the job of seeing to it that a large geographical area, in many cases a whole state, knows what we know about a personal relationship with Christ. And if in your parish you have found new life and power you will want everyone to have the same opportunity.

But how can the Bishop provide this opportunity in the dozens of villages and rural areas where there are not enough people to support a priest to lead and teach and nourish them in the kind of experience you have in your parish? There is no difference between your parish and a country mission except that you have enough money to pay your own way and they don't. The Bishop must ask the "haves" to make it possible for the "have-nots" to have leadership. He must count on your partnership; he must know that you see the Church as something larger than your parish, with the same goals everywhere that you have at home.

In the second place, in all ways except the financial, the Bishop wants to help your parish, too. He has just as much pastoral concern for your parish as for any other part of the diocese. He wants your parish life to be strong and deep. To help him help you and the others, he has a "vestry" acting as his assistants. This vestry is called, usually, the executive council of the diocese. It is elected by the annual diocesan convention, as your Vestry is elected by your annual parish meeting.

This council divides, as perhaps your Vestry does, into such areas of special interest as Christian education, Christian social relations, and so on. The function of these divisions, or departments, is to serve you. They provide specialists, ready at all times to come into your parish and help you deal with problems that are troubling you in some aspect of your parish life. Alone, you could not afford this service. But when all the parishes of the diocese join in paying for it, everyone can have it at a minimum cost.

Thirdly, by this same sharing of expense, you and the other parishes can combine to set up certain institutions—homes for the aged, summer camps, schools, and other such facilities— that no one parish could support by itself but which can be maintained by all of you together.

A quotation from Bishop Bayne pulls it all together perfectly. "A diocese," he says, "is the smallest unit of the Church. A parish is a fraction, not a unit, but a diocese is a family in the Christian household. The bishop is not at the *top* of the diocesan structure; he's always at the *heart*. The rest of the diocesan family gathers around him."

The diocese is not "they." It is all of you joining together, around the Bishop, to extend your ministry beyond your own parish, to strengthen your fraction by the use of a staff of specially trained consultants, and to make possible certain institutional services.

Once you have seen the diocese as the unit and the diocesan program as a joint ministry of all its fractions, rather than the mysterious doings of a little group of strangers in the Bishop's office, you cannot escape seeing your relation to it. You are a participant and not just a taxpayer. It is your Vestry's responsibility to know the details of what the diocese is doing, to make effective use of the services it offers, to see that your parishioners understand it from your point of view, and to make the voice of your parish heard in diocesan program planning.

The two direct ways of being involved in diocesan planning are to have a member of your parish on the executive council and to speak up in the diocesan convention. The council is small, however, and in the normal course of things you will have someone on it only once every few years. The convention, on the other hand, is so big and its agenda usually so stereotyped that it is difficult to be effective there.

What, then, is the answer? The best one is to establish year-round contacts with the diocesan staff. Invite them, on a regularly scheduled basis, to come into your parish, to meet with your Vestry, to speak to your people, and to work with your special interest groups. In a recent survey, a majority of Vestrymen said they believed their difficulties with the diocese would be overcome if members of the diocesan staff would visit the parish more often. And indeed they would.

And even though the executive council and the diocesan convention offer scant opportunity for you to make any creative contribution to the planning, you will find that the personal contacts and casual conversations you have with these diocesan staff people will provide a setting in which the voice of your parish will be heard with real effect. Your best participation in the life of the diocese will be on this intimate, informal basis.

The Diocesan Convention: Some dioceses call it a "convocation" and some call it a "council," but under one name or another every diocese has an annual meeting attended by all clergy and some number (determined by diocesan Canon) of lay delegates from each parish and mission.

Your delegates may or may not be Vestrymen—usually some are and some are not. (Your diocesan Canon tells how your delegates are elected. There is no national uniformity on this.)

We have been saying in this chapter that your relationship with the diocese is not a matter of "they" and "we." Your delegates go to the convention as your representatives—yes, but not in the spirit of defending your parish against some remote, detached "they." This is your annual formal participation in the affairs of the larger Church family to which you belong. Your delegates and all the others are meeting primarily as the Church, not as protectors of their local interests.

It is something like the Senate. A Senator does indeed represent a constituency back in Ohio or Colorado or wherever, but first of all he is a United States Senator bound by oath to try to take the total view.

Whether your delegates are Vestrymen or not, it is up to the Vestry to see that they are briefed on the agenda of the convention. Most dioceses nowadays provide the parish with a copious preview of the agenda. When you receive this, get your delegates together, with the Rector present, of course, and go through it in general discussion. It is not in keeping with an attitude of diocesan unity for your delegates to be instructed as to how to vote. They must have freedom of mind and conscience to listen to the debate and vote according to their judgment as to the total good. Nevertheless, they should know the mind of the parish on the matters that will be brought up.

It is absolutely necessary that the Vestry, at its next meeting after the convention, or at a special meeting, hear a report from the delegates. There may or may not be items of information you will want to pass on to your people. That is for you to decide. But you yourselves *must* have a firsthand account of what happened.

7 YOU AND THE NATIONAL CHURCH

JUST AS your diocese has its "vestry," called the diocesan council, bishop and council, or executive council, so does the whole American Episcopal Church have a vestry, which is known as "The Executive Council of the Episcopal Church." It consists of forty-five members (bishops, clergymen, and lay men and women) elected variously by the General Convention, the Women's Triennial Meeting, and the provinces. It meets four times a year to do exactly the same things your Vestry does: set policy, determine activities, and deal with finance.

The diocese, we have said, is the smallest unit of the Church. The national Church is the next smallest, or next largest, depending on the direction from which you are looking at it. The largest from our own Anglican point of view is the whole Anglican Communion, but don't forget that beyond even that there is the whole Christian Church—Baptists, Roman Catholics, Presbyterians, Methodists, Orthodox, and all the others who together make up God's one great Church. This is what the Ecumenical Movement is about: the recognition that all Christians, in spite of their temperamental, aesthetic, and theological diversities, form God's one great task force. You are an officer in that, too.

(We skip over the province here because the province has not yet found itself in the life of our American Church. There are eight provinces, geographical divisions of the Episcopal Church in the United States. At present they are mainly units of geographical convenience with little status and less power, but the time will undoubtedly come when they will have more importance. Normally, in our thinking, the mind jumps from diocese to National Church.)

Probably the work of the Executive Council seems terribly remote to you. And admittedly you have little opportunity for personal participation in it. Nevertheless, it is the program of the Church, of which your parish is a fraction, and as a Vestryman it is up to you to have a grasp of what it is doing in our country and around the world. Some of its departments serve your diocese, and therefore serve you. Others represent you in the ministry of the Church in regions where you cannot possibly exercise your ministry personally.

For many years the Executive Council operated through the following departments and divisions: Overseas, Home, Christian Social Relations, Christian Education, Communication, Finance, General Division of Women's Work, General Division of Laymen's Work, and the General Division of Research and Field Study. As the Presiding Bishop pointed out, this structure was weak in the area of decision-making, clear definition of responsibility, and ability to respond promptly and effectively to rapidly changing conditions in the Church. And all these weaknesses were accentuated by the first two factors.

Under the reorganization, the Executive Council now functions through a Staff Program Group (SPG), of which the Presiding Bishop is chairman, assisted by a Deputy for Program and a Deputy for Overseas Relations, with the Director of Financial Services and the Director of Communication as advisory members. The Ecumenical Officer and the Bishop for the Armed Forces are attached to the office of the Presiding Bishop. The four units of SPG are Service to Dioceses, Professional Leadership Development, Experimental and Specialized Services, and General Convention Special Program. Bishop Hines has emphasized that this structure will be on a trial basis for probably two years and constantly subject to adjustment. The effectiveness of the changes will be thoroughly evaluated at the end of the trial period.

As officially announced, the functions and responsibilities of SPG, the deputies, and the units are outlined on the next four pages.

FUNCTIONS AND RESPONSIBILITIES
OF THE
STAFF PROGRAM GROUP

- To function as the central point of decision, coordination, and integration for all staff activities related to the General Church Program.

- To propose to the Executive Council strategic directions and new programs.

- To assure and achieve central planning on behalf of the Executive Council.

Deputy for Program

1. To be the Presiding Bishop's chief executive officer.

2. Responsible for:

    - Chairing the SPG in the absence of the Presiding Bishop

    - Executing through SPG the policies, objectives, priorities, and directives of the Executive Council

    - Developing SPG policies and proposals for submission to the Executive Council

    - Assuring effective communication between program units and the Presiding Bishop

    - Assuring effective response by the program units to requests from the Deputy for Overseas Relations, Commissions of General Convention, and other official Church bodies.

Deputy for Overseas Relations

1. Planning and strategy with non-U.S. Churches.

2. Relationship with and care of overseas personnel.

3. Communication and Extrabudgetary support.

4. Anglican and other ecumenical overseas Church relationships.

THE UNITS

I. Service to Dioceses

To provide coordinated, unified services and resources to dioceses for strengthening their programs of mission, ministry, and education.

1. Range of services/resources to assist *them* to coordinate the use of. . .

2. Lay education and training (assist dioceses).

3. Two-way communication—hear and respond.

4. Innovation and development for lay leadership, diocesan planning, and ecumenical action.

II. *Professional Leadership Development*

To be a center for reflection, information, evaluation, and improvement of professional personnel education, training, deployment, and care.

1. Studies, theological reflections, training facility, evaluation, and communication strategy.

2. Provide qualified overseas and specialized personnel.

3. Strengthen theological education and professional training.

4. Develop systems of professional deployment and rehabilitation.

III. *Experimental and Specialized Services*

To test and develop new methods and structures and improve services to special needs.

1. Conduct experimentation and evaluation and develop results.

2. Anticipate future specific needs.

3. Interpret Church's position on public issues.

4. Consultation services to specialized institutions.

5. Develop and support special services to persons and groups in need.

IV. General Convention Special Program

1. To help the poor gain voice and power.

2. To aid the Church in eliminating racism and responding to the needs of the poor.

3. To encourage use of power for justice and self-determination.

For more detailed information about the work of the Executive Council, write to The Episcopal Church Center, 815 Second Avenue, New York, New York 10017.

8 THE COMMISSION SYSTEM

As PARISHES everywhere move away from their old self-image as private clubs and more and more look outward to the surrounding community as the field of their ministry, an interesting new way of organizing the Vestry has come into being. Various names are used to describe this plan, but here we shall call it the Commission System.

In principle and in practice it is extremely simple. The first step is to determine the aspects of your parish life that require special and continuous attention. It can be expected that you will come up with a list of such concerns as worship, education, social relations, missions, property, finance, and perhaps others according to what you see to be local needs.

The Vestry and Rector appoint a Vestryman to head a commission on each of these special activities. The Vestryman then draws upon the total membership of the parish to form his commission. (Here the first advantage of the system shows up: maximum lay participation in parish life. The head of the commission can, according to the ramifications of his assignment, involve many parishioners in his particular part of the action of the parish.)

Suppose, as an illustration, you are made head of the Worship Commission. This may be the trickiest example we could have chosen, for after all the Rector is really in charge of all worship services and does not have to take advice or suggestions from anyone. But suppose anyhow that your Rector sees the value and welcomes the help of a Worship Commission. You will need quite a few people on your team. Your commission will have responsibility for the altar guild, its training and functioning, for the choir, the ushers, the acolytes, and for the lay readers. You will surround yourself with several subcommittees and quite a body of responsible workers. Note how this approach takes these necessary functions out of the hands of one frustrated, long-suffering person here and there, unifies these people and the others whom you will add into an integrated whole, each of whom feels a personal stake in a smoothly running totality.

Another, less loaded, example would be the Education Commission. Suppose you are appointed head of that. Here you have responsibility at least for the Church school, the young people's group, and for all the adult education activities the parish should have. This is no one-man job. You will have to enlist all the help you can get, and a large number of people will be involved.

The Vestryman who heads the Social Relations Commission will have to have a subcommittee that deals with the local council of churches, and one that identifies itself with community social agencies and with the diocesan Department of Christian Social Relations. This latter subcommittee will perhaps divide further, according to the variety of agencies and activities. Many people will be needed for this commission.

Some of the parishes that use this system have what they call a Fellowship Commission. You may have an objection to the worn-out word "fellowship," but the purpose of such a commission is clear, and so is the need for one, perhaps called by some less trite name. There are few parishes so small that everyone knows everyone else, and fewer where the members have that sense of being a "community of the forgiven and the forgiving" that is the foundation of real parish life. Then, too, in the mobility of modern life, every parish always has its newcomers to be assimilated into the parish family. The Vestryman who heads such a commission has a subtle, intangible task before him. We are not talking here about the contrived cordiality of so many ushers or the charm of the friendly neighborhood Rector. Nor are we talking about the dreary hospitality of the coffee hour. This is a purposeful fraternizing. The Vestryman will need a corps of sensitive persons around him who will be able to see beyond mere sociability and plan to draw their people and the strangers in their midst into an awareness of their corporate unity as a Christian group.

The functions of a Finance Commission are obvious. The Vestryman at the head of this commission will need many helpers for the Every Member Canvass alone. If, as he certainly should, he tries to pull together the scattered funds of the parish and to set up a Finance Committee as suggested on page 49, he will perforce call upon a still larger number of laity.

An Evangelism Commission may or may not appeal to you. There is some disagreement in the Church about just what evangelism is. Some say it is getting out and bringing people into the Church; others say it is creating an inner parish life of such quality that people will be irresistibly drawn to it. In either case it is arranging that individuals have an encounter with Jesus Christ, and probably both sides of the argument have their merits. It is a little like the sales and production departments of a business firm each insisting that the other is nonessential. Some parishes do have an Evangelism Commission. The Vestryman in charge of this one could conceivably enlist everyone in the parish.

A Property Commission needs no explanation. Here the skills of many members of the parish can be put to work. The material fabric can be kept in top condition at minimum expense by the enlistment of members who have special training in the necessary crafts.

You can add to the list of appropriate commissions according to what you see to be your needs. You decide what commissions you ought to have. But don't trump any up. It is worse to give someone an unconvincing job in the Church than to give him none at all. It makes the Church seem trivial to him.

Besides its assurance of maximum lay participation in parish life, there are these other advantages to the Commission System:

1. Every Vestry meeting becomes a review of the total parish picture. As the head of each commission makes his report and talks about his special problems, all the other Vestrymen get a living view of this one facet of the parish operation. The Vestrymen counsel and plan with one another, and by the time all reports are made and discussed everyone at the meeting is up to the minute on the state of the whole parish.

2. Each man and woman in the parish finds opportunity to work in the area of his or her own special interest and abilities. (This is also of advantage to the Vestryman as he sets up his commission. People are much more easily and effectively enlisted when they are asked to do something congenial to their already established concerns.)

I have heard only two objections to the Commission System, and both seem readily answerable.

Some say a Parish Council accomplishes the same things without all the clanking of so much official machinery. And indeed the Parish Council idea is much like the Commission

System. The one important difference is that the Commission System puts the authority and responsibility where they belong, in the hands of the elected leadership of the parish. The Vestry has status; the Parish Council has none. Also, it is true that many a Parish Council is created mainly in an effort to bypass a do-nothing Vestry or with the mistaken idea that the Vestry is concerned only with the financial part of parish life. If what you want is a Parish Council, why not set up one that has official status and power by organizing your Vestry on the lines of the Commission System?

The other misgiving that has been expressed is that there is no assurance that the persons elected to the Vestry will be the right ones to head the necessary commissions. The answer here is in two parts: first, if a Vestryman is appointed to head a commission for which other people have better qualifications, he naturally conscripts these other people as a sort of executive or advisory board. Secondly, parishes that have used the Commission System over a period of years report that the people very soon begin to elect men and women of special competence to the Vestry.

We dealt with your relations with the people of the parish in Chapter V, and promised that we would show how to take out much of the present vagueness of that relationship. For this purpose, the Commission System is an excellent instrument. As head of a commission you have a meaningful association with a number of parishioners within a definite context, and so does every other Vestryman. As a whole Vestry, you will reach practically the entire parish in the creative kind of contacts that always develop when people work together in a common cause.

9 PARISH FINANCES

EPISCOPALIANS like to be witty about the way parishes handle their finances. A speaker can always get a laugh by saying the Church must be a divine institution because if it weren't it would have been bankrupt long ago. Or he can quote Bishop Lawrence's old riddle: When is a businessman not a businessman? Answer: When he is a Vestryman.

These alleged jokes were not funny even when they were new. Church business, including the financial part of it, is the Lord's business. Carelessness about it is not material for wisecracks.

Parish finances can easily be put in order and kept so. Most Vestrymen are businessmen. They know how books should be set up and expenditures controlled. They know how a picture of the current situation can be kept always available. It is reasonable to suppose that the Lord expects them to use in his business the same skill, judgment, and analytical know-how they use in their own.

But the fact is that the monetary affairs of far too many parishes are in deplorable shape. Plausible reasons can be offered for this. It is partly because the income is not constant. Pledges lag, Christmas and Easter offerings beguile us into a false sense of prosperity, the biggest contributor moves away, and so on. It is also partly because expenses are not entirely predictable. Heating plants break down, organs get out of whack, and roofs develop leaks. The devil thinks up all sorts of emergencies. These are our excuses. But the same things happen in your own business, don't they? Don't you have delinquent accounts, peak seasons, and the possible loss of your best customer to consider? Don't you have emergencies? Of course you do, and you make intelligent provision for such facts of business life.

As basic essentials to orderly procedure, we can take realistic budgeting and careful bookkeeping for granted. Most parishes seem to do an acceptable job in both of these particulars.

Where they run into trouble is in the month-to-month analysis of their situation, both as to income and expenditures. I have known parishes where the Treasurer's monthly report at the Vestry meeting consisted of three totals: income this month, expenses this month, balance on hand—all jotted down on the back of an envelope. I have also seen elaborate itemizations of both income and outgo for the month, combined with a bare statement of balance on hand. The two were equally useless. Neither the minutely detailed one nor the one on the envelope told the Vestry anything about how they stood in relation to the rest of the year.

In one of these parishes the result of such reporting was that after Easter, when the Easter offering made the balance on hand deceptively large, the Vestry went on a spending spree. Then when the lean months of summer came, they had to borrow money to meet their obligations. So they borrowed it from the endowment, "After all, we are only borrowing from ourselves, you know." In a little more than ten years, the entire parish endowment fund consisted of notes signed by the Vestry.

The cure for such slaphappy management is so simple one wonders why every parish doesn't just naturally think of it. All you need is a monthly trial balance which, in addition to what happened last month, also shows what should have happened so far this year, what actually has happened, and how far you are ahead or behind on each budget item.

The Executive Council's Department of Finance recommends that it be done as shown on the following two pages.

One special advantage of this form is that it follows exactly the Executive Council's Parish Cash Book, from which items can be transferred directly to your annual report. The Cash Book is available from Seabury Press, 815 Second Avenue, New York 17, New York.

In every parish at least once a year the Vestry should see a report of special funds (see form p. 52). In larger parishes where there is considerable activity in these funds, the treasurer should make the report often enough to keep the Vestry up to date.

Finance Committee: A good device used in many parishes is that of the Finance Committee, which meets a day or two before or a few hours before the Vestry meeting, reviews the financial statement, and reports to the Vestry. This is a tremendous timesaver. A great deal of time is often wasted at Vestry meetings over minor matters that could be anticipated and investigated by the Finance Committee and resolved in its report. Another timesaver is to give the Property (or Maintenance) Committee authority to spend within the limits of its own budget without requiring Vestry action on each individual expenditure.

If everything is all right, the Finance Committee so reports, and that is that. If there are matters that need Vestry discussion or action, the committee says so, makes its suggestions, and you go on from there.

Besides helping the Vestry clear away a lot of debris, a

Note: these forms are guides on which your own forms can be modeled. They are not available otherwise.

PARISH TREASURER'S MONTHLY REPORT TO VESTRY
(prepared on the cash basis)

_____Parish at _____ Month of _____, 19_____

Dated _____ Signed_____Treasurer

RECEIPTS

		Month	Year to Date	Budget
	For Parish Support:			
1.	Plate collections	$...............	$...............	$...............
2.	Pledges and subscriptions	....	....	....
3.	Church school	....	....	....
4.	Parish organizations	....	....	....
5.	Other sources			
a.	....	....	....	....
b.	....	....	....	....
c.	....	....	....	....
d.	....	....	....	....
e.	....	....	....	....
6.	Investment income	....	....	....
	For Designated Parochial Purposes:	....	....	....
7.	Communion alms	....	....	....
8.	Designated gifts for the Parish	....	....	....
9.	Investment income	....	....	....
	For Work Outside Parish:	....	....	....
10.	Missionary and general church program	....	....	....
11.	Special offerings	....	....	....
	Legacies and Other Donations (non-recurring):	....	....	....
12.	Legacies and bequests	....	....	....
13.	Other donations to capital	....	....	....
14.	Capital gains (or losses)	....	....	....
15.	Sale of Investments or Property (incl. savings accounts)	....	....	....
16.	Money Borrowed	....	....	....
17.	Exchanges	....	....	....
	TOTAL RECEIPTS:	$_____	$_____	$_____

SUMMARY

	Month	Year to Date	Budget
Total Receipts (per above)	$...............	$...............	$...............
Total Disbursements (per page 2)	_____	_____	_____
Excess (Deficit) of Receipts over Disbursements	$...............	$...............	$...............
Add Beginning Bank Balance	_____	_____	_____
Bank Balance — End of Period (see below)	$_____	$_____	$_____

ALLOCATION OF CASH FUNDS

Checking account — allocated to Special Funds (see page 3) . $...............
 — available for general parish purposes . ...
Total (per above) . . . . . . $...............
Savings accounts — allocated to Special Funds (see page 3) . ...
 — available for general parish purposes . . _____

$_____

PARISH TREASURER'S MONTHLY REPORT TO VESTRY

DISBURSEMENTS

	For Current Expenses — Parish:	Month	Year to Date	Budget
18.	Salaries:			
a.	Rector's salary	$	$	$
b.				
c.				
d.				
e.				
f.				
19.	Social security taxes			
20.	Insurance premiums			
21.	Fuel, light, water and power			
22a.	Office supplies and postage			
22b.	Church school supplies			
23.	Auto and travel expense			
24.	Telephone and telegraph			
25.	Altar supplies			
26.	Music, choir supplies and maintenance			
27.	Bookkeeping and auditing			
28.	Other parish expense			
	TOTAL CURRENT EXPENSE	$	$	$
L-29.	Pension Premiums			
M-30.	Diocesan Assessments			
	For Special Parochial Purposes:			
31.	Communion Alms			
32.	Rental property expense			
33.				
34.	Chapel or parochial mission expense			
35.	Repairs and minor improvements			
36.	Interest paid			
37.	Taxes			
38.	Rent			
39.	Other special parochial purposes			
	Diocesan and General Church Missionary Program:			
40.	Missionary Fund assessments			
41.	Special offerings			
42.	Major Improvements and Additions to Property			
43.	Purchase of Investments (incl. Savings Accts.)			
44.	Payments on Loans — principal			
45.	Exchanges			
	TOTAL DISBURSEMENTS	$	$	$

PARISH TREASURER'S MONTHLY REPORT TO VESTRY

REPORT OF SPECIAL FUNDS

For the period _____, 19____ to_____, 19____

Name of Fund	Cash in Bank				Investments (1) and Savings Accounts (2)	Total Fund _____, 19____
	Beginning Balance _____, 19___	Receipts	Disbursements	Ending Balance _____, 19___		
	$................	$................	$................	$................	$................	$................
	....	....	....	....	....	....
	....	....	....	....	....	....
	....	....	....	....	....	....
	....	....	....	....	....	....
	....	....	....	....	....	....
	....	....	....	....	....	....
	....	....	....	....	....	....
	....	....	....	....	....	....
	....	....	....	....	....	....
	....	....	....	....	....	....
	....	....	....	....	....	....
	....	....	....	....	....	....
	....	....	....	....	....	....
	....	....	....	....	....	....
	....	....	....	....	....	....
	....	....	....	....	....	....
	....	....	....	....	....	....
	....	....	....	....	....	....
	....	....	....	....	....	....
	....	....	....	....	....	....
	....	....	....	....	....	....
	....	....	....	....	....	....
	....	....	....	....	....	....
	$_____	$_____	$_____	$_____	$_____	$_____

Total Investments $................(1)
Total Savings Accounts   _____(2)

$_____

Finance Committee also provides a method of involving more people of the parish in an intimate, up-to-date knowledge of parish finances. The treasurer should, of course, be chairman of the Finance Committee.

Endowments: A certain amount of argument goes on about whether or not an endowment is good for a parish. Some say it makes a parish lazy. And some say it gives the parish the ability, to use Bishop Sherrill's famous phrase, "to strike with power."

It all depends on how the endowment is used. It is quite possible, and we have all seen it happen, for a parish to sit back on its endowment while its responsibility, imagination, interest, and finally its very life all just dwindle away.

But I can also tell you of a parish that suddenly inherited a million dollars and by right use of the income became a mighty force. The parishioners separated their legacy from the regular parish funds and said, "We will use the income for good purposes outside our parish. We will devote it as wisely as we can to Overseas Missions." (It could have been something else. They happened to select missions.)

So they have a year-round program to educate themselves about where money can best be used in the overseas work of the Church. They study. They invite overseas bishops and missionaries to come and tell them about their work and needs. They learn all they can about the whole missionary field; at the end of the year they meet, informed and concerned, to divide the interest on a million dollars among the places where they think it will do the most good.

Here is an endowment that is twice blessed: "it blesses him that gives and him that takes."

The problem about endowments is not whether they are good or not. The only problem is how they are used.

One Treasurer—or Several: There is a growing trend toward having all money pass through the hands of the Parish

Treasurer (though some dioceses require that there be a separate treasurer for missions).

The old custom has been for each organization in the parish, even the Church school, to have its own treasurer, handling the funds raised by the organization itself. The women's group, youth group, men's club, boy scout troop, and others beyond number, have had bazaars, dances, pancake suppers, and so on, each organization collecting a little or a lot of money and spending it according to its special interests. And each has kept its own books, proud of its autonomy, reporting only to the annual Parish Meeting, which has no power to do anything but offer polite, bored applause as each treasurer reads his mysterious statistics about the financial vicissitudes of his little band during the past year.

The first fact that jumps out at you from this situation is that it makes any pretense of parish unity completely ridiculous. It actively encourages the parish to divide into a number of unrelated units, each with a life of its own, unaware of its place in the total purpose. I have known people who said, "I do not want to be on the parish mailing list. My interest is in St. Swithin's Guild."

Secondly, such a situation diverts each group from its stated *raison d'être* into a concentration on money raising.

These two facts have struck many parishes with a sudden glaring illumination. Again, we are talking about parishes that understand their true function. Such parishes have seen that the whole membership marches as a single unit. They have seen that organizations exist only for worship, teaching, and service and are therefore integral parts of the parish's total program and should not be required to spend time financing themselves. Everything the parish does should be paid for out of the general budget.

You think at once of the many parishes in which organizational money-raising efforts are necessary to supplement the general budget. This applies especially to the women's organizations. Some parishes are dependent on the proceeds from the women's activities. This simply should not be. It is part of our failure to understand the nature of the Church.

Neither the women, nor any other group, should raise money. This is a new idea, but not brand-new. The Right Rev. Daniel Corrigan tells of a parish he had, before he was consecrated Bishop five years ago, where no organizations raised money. People organized for service, and the parish budget financed them.

Each year these groups appear before the Vestry and present their programs for the coming year. Some have programs of serving the aged in the community, some work in the local mental hospital, the VA hospital, and the terminal cancer hospital. These are only examples of the various community activities of this parish.

Over one-third of the parish budget goes to support such projects, and, says Bishop Corrigan, "It is subscribed without difficulty."

The results of such a policy are electrifying. This one simple reorganization of parish finance changes the entire focus of parish activity.

We have grown old and hard in our ways of keeping the parish above water financially by any possible means. We will find it very difficult to change over to the view that we are financing task forces rather than an institution. We have over many years developed "church workers," whose tireless loyalty found expression in the drudgery of "keeping the place going." Through the pettiness of our understanding we have cheated them out of the fullness of their true ministry by limiting their opportunities to "church work" rather than the work of the Church.

A sad letter comes to my mind; I received it from a parish that had, by a highly successful tithing campaign, reached a position of such affluence that special money-raising activities were no longer necessary. "Our parish is falling apart," the writer said. Could I suggest a program for a parish that had no financial problems?

What would you have told them? The only answer is that they must now for the first time take the trouble to learn the true function of a parish.

10 THE EVERY MEMBER CANVASS

NOT LONG AGO a highly successful businessman who also happens to be a Vestryman said to one of his fellow Vestrymen, "We have to plan for this Every Member Canvass but let's face it: it's a job no one really likes to do." If that sounds like someone you know, the chances are you are right. It could have happened in almost any Vestry meeting. Yet the man's appraisal of the Every Member Canvass is less true today than it may have been just a few short years ago. Throughout the Church there are signs of growing maturity in our approach to giving. One of these signs is the tone the Every Member Canvass is assuming in more and more parishes.

The Every Member Canvass came into being in the United States fairly early in the twentieth century. It appeared on the scene when the country and the Church were enchanted by techniques of getting on with the job more efficiently. It was the age when a book called *The Salesman from Galilee* could be written and rather widely acclaimed.

Into this climate came the first Every Member Canvass. It was efficient, businesslike, tidy, and in tune with the times. It took the budget of the Church to the people. It organized the men of the Church into teams with captains. They were told they were "salesmen" and "sales managers" and, since this was the language of the day, they readily accepted these roles. The canvass was approached with the enthusiasm we all have for something new. Gradually therefore—because the appeal of novelty does not last long—it fell into the class of a chore to be done by a handful of the faithful and avoided by the more fleet of foot. Some, who still see this early image of the canvass, say they hope to see it disappear entirely some day.

That day may come, but there are many in the Church who are not quite ready to believe that it is here yet. To hope for the day when the high-pressure tone and the "salesmen" and "prospects" approach disappear is another thing entirely. That day cannot come too soon. There are signs that it is coming rapidly.

The Every Member Canvass is one of the few occasions in the year when the whole parish family has the opportunity to talk over its condition and its goals—as a family. The caller makes his visits to tell those on whom he calls about the parish's concerns at that moment, to hear what the person being called on has to say about them, and to ask support.

The primary concern of the canvass is stewardship. By that is meant the way the members of the Christian family are managing the time, the talent, and the money God has entrusted to them—as individuals and as a parish. When the caller asks for a financial pledge, he is not asking for money alone. He is asking another member of the family to decide and declare his part in all this. The pledge is but one measure of stewardship. It is a unique measure because money is, in a very real way, the person. He gave part of his life in exchange for it, and what he does with it is a good indicator of what he thinks that much of his life was worth. As he pledges his money—he is pledging himself.

The point of the canvass call, therefore, is really a point of decision. Every family needs this sort of deadline for decision.

That is why the parish conducts an Every Member Canvass, and does it year after year.

The old out-and-out budget support canvass where the parish was mentally (if not actually) divided into salesmen and prospects, where the emphasis was solely on money to meet the budget, is disappearing. Few there be who will mourn its passing. In its place there is developing a program of lay visitation, in which the discussion of money, while playing an important part, is being set against a background of broader, deeper teaching of Christian stewardship.

As the Every Member Canvass fits into a program of year-round stewardship, teaching it is quite a different thing from the high-powered "let's get on with it" budget support venture of its early years. Even then the canvass was not all bad. Its element of having Christians call on other Christians in their homes to talk about money and the Church was good. But what the canvasser was encouraged to say and the way he was to look at the family on whom he called, were at times somewhat less than Christian.

The tone and the emphasis have changed. Many in the Church see stewardship as a way of life by which the Christian is taught to handle all of his time, his ability, and his material possessions as trusts from God. More and more (although not nearly enough) the Church's teaching of Christian steward-ship is being preached about all through the year. The Christian's responsibility to exercise his stewardship in all areas of his daily life is being discussed in adult groups. In many congregations the word "stewardship" is not being saved only to be used to make an annual financial appeal more palatable. The Church knows that it cannot put stewardship into a neat little box and tie it into a tidy package. Nor can it measure the depth of stewardship with a rule calibrated in dollar signs. Such a measure is far too small.

It is this broader and deeper concept of Christian stewardship that is today being incorporated into more and more canvass training sessions. Set against such a background the canvass is no secular intrusion into the spiritual life of the parish. It is rather the occasion when men and women of the parish can call on each other in their homes to consider one, but only one, phase of their Christian stewardship—how much of their material income they will set aside for the Church. As they consider this responsibility they will be doing so within the context of their total responsibility to handle all their time, ability, and possessions as trusts from God to be used as he would have them used.

An Every Member Canvass that measures up to these terms is a matter very much for Vestry concern. As partners with your Rector in the administrative matters of the parish, and in setting the tone of parish life generally, you will want very much to have a strong hand in determining the tone and direction of the Every Member Canvass. It has a vital role to play in the spiritual and physical well-being of your parish. It merits the best talent and effort that can be put into it.

If the Every Member Canvass gives Christians an opportunity to talk together as members of the same Christian family in these terms; if it sets pledging to the Church in the right perspective; if it enables the Church to interpret the right motives for Christian giving; if the canvassers understand that their task is more than simply raising money; if planning and training for an Every Member Canvass mean that a significant number of men and women will be talking with each other about responsible handling of their resources—you do not really want to get rid of it, do you?

A word of caution to avoid disappointment. No matter how well you plan, how carefully you train your canvassers, some will not grasp the full significance of this opportunity for spiritual adventure. Let's not give it up because of that.

One out of twelve of the first band of followers missed the point of Christianity!

If your canvass has been floundering or is wearing thin or is being looked on as a chore to be ducked, before you give it up —examine the basis on which it has been presented. You can make it a spiritual experience that will enrich the life of the parish. It is doing so in many parishes. Thank God for our growing maturity.

11 THE ANNUAL PARISH MEETING

EVERY PARISH is required by diocesan Canon to hold an annual meeting. This is the one big opportunity for all the people to get together to discuss the state of the parish, to make themselves individually heard about its program and activities, to elect its Vestrymen, and to hear and ask questions about what its component parts have done over the past year.

This sounds rather important, and it certainly is. You would expect that any serious member, concerned about the ministry of his parish, would let nothing keep him away from such a source of information and such a forum for personal expression.

Well, maybe that's what you would think if you did not know about Parish Meetings. The facts, which can be documented by a recent questionnaire, show how it really is:

Average attendance at Parish Meetings is 21.9 per cent of the parishioners eligible to vote. (Eligibility is determined by your diocesan Canon.)

Little attempt is made in any parish to promote attendance. Usually, the Rector makes an announcement from the chancel, and a notice is carried in the Sunday bulletin, and that is all.

Very few parishes make any effort to give tempo or coherence to the meeting. They simply list the agenda items, with the implication that these are the tiresome chores we have to wade through.

The election of Vestrymen is usually a cut-and-dried affair. The nominations of the Nominating Committee go through without a hitch. (Only about half the nominees have been consulted beforehand about their willingness to accept election.)

In short, the average Parish Meeting is a dull, dry, unplanned, unimaginative bore. Only a handful of the dutiful show up. I can personally remember a time—in a diocese where the canonical quorum was, bitterly but realistically, fixed at eighteen—when some of those present had to go out and round up a few more in order to hold the meeting at all.

That's the way it is, but it certainly does not have to be so. There is no reason why the Parish Meeting cannot be an exciting annual climax in the cycle of parish life. All you need is planning and promotion.

A notice should go by mail to every home in the parish, and should be followed by a telephone call.

A dinner should precede the meeting. It can be paid for out of the parish budget; a charge can be made; it can be "potluck"; or an offering can be taken. People should be seated at small tables, six or eight to each table. Before the dinner one couple should be assigned to each table to act as host and hostess to see that, if there are newcomers among the group, everyone gets acquainted and to keep conversation going. (Do not make some of the women cook the dinner and thereby be relegated to the kitchen. They belong in the meeting.)

The endless list of required reports can be cut down. Some that are purely statistical in nature, like the Rector's report on how many services of various kinds he has held, can be mimeographed and put beside the people's places at the tables.

Others that have to do with persons and activities can, with a little imagination, perhaps he dramatized. A part of the Planning Committee's job is to figure out how to liven up these reports ordinarily so perfunctory and so deadly.

When it comes to the election of Vestrymen, there should be a feeling of freedom to make nominations from the floor. In any sizable parish a Nominating Committee is a necessity, but any individual member of the parish has every right in the world to add to that list. (He should know that his candidate is available.)

Naturally, you will get some ill-advised nominations. People are always thinking: "If we put Mr. Soandso on the Vestry we might get him interested" or "Mr. Whatshisname's wife (or mother) has been such a faithful worker, and it would please her so much if we elected him." Large pledgers and men of social status are also likely to be nominated and to get some votes regardless of their qualifications. There is not a thing you can do about this. The parish family operates by the democratic process, and you have to rely on the common sense of the majority.

It is good timing to begin the business of the evening with the Vestry election. It gives your tellers time to count the votes and report the results at the end of the meeting.

All this is the barest outline of ways to improve your Parish Meeting. It could not possibly make specific suggestions about how your own parish will want to put meat on this skeleton with discussions and ideas about program, thoughts about where your ministry needs strengthening, a statement from the Rector about how he sees the total picture, and that sort of thing. Only you know about your local interests and problems.

But it must be obvious that some such reforms will do a great deal toward making your Parish Meeting something more than just the tolerated burden it probably is now.

Customarily, the Rector is chairman of the Parish Meeting.

12 CALLING A
NEW RECTOR

Suppose your Rector has resigned. Did you know you don't have to accept his resignation? Canon 45 definitely says that, with a few special exceptions noted in Canon 44, "a Rector may not resign his Parish without the consent of the said Parish."

Once in a long while one hears of a parish that says, "We can't let you leave us"; there is always something thrilling about hearing that, but it doesn't happen very often. Perhaps this is partly because most Vestries do not know it *can* happen.

But suppose, as is usually the case, you have accepted his resignation and, with appropriate expressions of how he will be missed, have congratulated him on his "advancement." Now what do you do?

According to Canon 46, it is all very simple.

1. The Wardens, or other proper officers (not defined) give notice to the Bishop that the vacancy exists.

2. You find another man you want, tell the Bishop you propose to elect him, and if the Bishop does not object within thirty days, you go ahead and elect him.

3. The Wardens give the Bishop *handwritten* notice that the election has taken place.

So much for the mechanics. It all sounds so nice and easy. No hint anywhere of the upheaval, the turmoil, the groping, the rows, the chaos, and the frustrations that can turn a parish upside down as it goes through the travail of bringing forth a new Rector.

Let's go into the considerations the Canon so nonchalantly leaves out.

In the first place, how do you know where to start looking for another clergyman? The thing to do immediately is to appoint a Nominating Committee and let its members do the looking. On this committee there should be some Vestrymen and some who are not Vestrymen. There should certainly be some women, and a responsible representative of the youth of the parish.

This committee must first be provided with certain information. They must know what your parish offers materially: salary, living facilities, allowances, etc. They must be able to answer questions about the opportunities and the needs of both your parish and your community.

It is in the briefing of the Nominating Committee that decisions are usually made about what age limits to set and "what kind of man we want," and more often than not these decisions are unwise if not naïve.

Advice to Nominating Committees: Nearly every parish specifies that it wants a young man. The situation seems to be getting a little better now, but there was a time not long ago when it was absurd. Some wag accused southern parishes of looking for ex-Confederate generals under thirty-five. Northern parishes were no different. Maturity, which one would suppose is absolutely essential in a leader, was a liability. Vestrymen were eager to call as their religious leaders men they would consider too young to take into their businesses on any but the lower echelons.

Many parishes now are willing to raise the age limit to

fifty-five, which is a big step in the right direction, but would still rule out nearly 20 per cent of the Church's 8500 clergymen, among whom might be just the man God wants in your parish. (The average age of our clergy is 43.8 years.)

Most parishes are just as superficial about other qualifications as they are about age. Everyone wants a good preacher, an attractive, energetic man, a man who gets along well with youth, a socially graceful man—the kind who will draw people and "make our church grow." Someone has said they look for a combination of Bob Hope and Phillips Brooks.

Also they want him to have an attractive—but not too attractive—wife.

Here again, in looking for a new Rector as in every other aspect of parish life, the true purpose of your parish is the crucial point around which all your considerations should center. You are looking for a priest of God who will lead and teach you and your people in a Spirit-motivated life. He might be ugly, awkward, sixty years old, and a terrible preacher and still be exactly the right man for you.

Your first resource for names is the Bishop. Your committee, or some of its representatives, should go to see him. And please don't think of this call on the Bishop as merely a courtesy call. Many committees have little intention of taking seriously any of the Bishop's nominations. To be just plain truthful about it, they don't trust him. They suspect that he may try to solve one of his own problems by foisting on them some man who is not getting along well in his present parish. Or they fear he does not understand the particular needs of their parish. "Our parish is unique." That is one thing that is true of all parishes; each one is unique.

Make no mistake about this. Your Bishop knows your parish much better than you think he does. And he knows his clergy. He of all people is in a position to match parish and man effectively. Moreover, he has a wide acquaintance with clergymen outside his diocese, and if his judgment tells him you should look outside, he can put you in touch with men you might otherwise never have heard of. Don't underrate the Bishop's stake in your search. It is to his interest that your parish have the right man.

Names will, you will find, pour in. Some clergymen will write to you and ask to be considered. In the Church this has always been thought of as bad taste, or a measure of desperation, or both, and there is enough basis for these feelings that such applications should be looked at with more than usual care. But don't just reject them out of hand. Our clergy-placement system is so bad as to be no system at all. There are good clergymen who do not have sufficient contacts to be able to depend upon someone else to sponsor their efforts to move.

Your own parishioners will give you many names. Some of the people who have come to you from other towns will nominate their former Rectors. Other parishioners will have acquaintances (and relatives) whom they will suggest. Clergy will send in names of friends of theirs. Your trouble will not be in developing a list, but in narrowing down the one you will find you have accumulated. This will be true whether your parish is great or obscure. The difference will be a matter of degree.

As to the problem of eliminating names, here the only answer is that you must be guided by your prayerful judgment and by your financial ability to go and talk with each man in his own bailiwick. Obviously, if you have a small parish in southern California, the cost of going to interview a man in Maine will be formidable.

But you *must* go to the man. If you ask him to come to preach in your parish and meet your people, the right kind of man will decline. He will tell you that unless he were called to be your Rector he could not possibly have any reason for seeing and being seen by your parish. (What he would mean is that it is beneath the dignity of a priest to "try out for a job.")

And when you do go to meet him, don't try to sneak in at the eleven o'clock service and taste his sermon with the illusion that he will not know you are there or what you are there for. There is no clergyman anywhere so guileless that he cannot spot a delegation from another parish the minute he sees one. The chances are all you will do will be to make him self-conscious and therefore see and hear him at his worst. At any rate, his sermon is no fair test of anything except perhaps his "stage presence." It is also true that if he is a good leader of his own congregation, the sermon may be so closely related to some local pastoral situation that it may be quite dull to you and yet vital to his own people. And the sermon, at best, is only a twenty-minute part of a clergyman's week, and it does not tell you anything about his other, and more important, qualifications.

A better thing to do is to write ahead to the man you are considering, tell him your parish is vacant and he has been suggested as a man who would meet your needs, and ask to have an hour or two with him alone, perhaps at a time other than Sunday morning. Then be entirely open about it. Tell him about your parish, and let him ask questions. Try to get to know him, and try to let him know you, not as shoppers, but as people who know what you are talking about.

Do not in any case ask him if he would accept if called. This is the ultimate imposition. If a young man said to a girl: "I have a list here of girls I am considering as matrimonial prospects. If, after seeing them all, I should decide to marry you, may I assume you will accept my proposal?" What do you think would happen? Whatever happened, he would have it coming to him.

From here on it is a process of making up your minds. Having screened out many of the nominations and having met and talked with the rest, you will come down to a few names you are ready to submit, ideally in the order of your preference.

The Canon does not say who does the calling, that is, who finally elects, but ordinarily it is the Vestry. In some dioceses, a parish meeting is required. In either case, the electing body receives the nominations and proceeds to an election, notifies the Bishop, and when the Bishop's approval is given, issues the call. Note that the Bishop's disapproval may, without violating the Canon, be disregarded.

There is always the chance, of course, that you may call every man on your list and not get an acceptance. So, you start over.

Your written call and the clergyman's written acceptance constitute a contract.

You see, there is no foolproof method of calling a Rector. It is a cumbersome, tedious, hit-and-miss process, full of chance and guesswork. There is no way you can meet all the clergymen who might be right for your parish and, if you could, there would still be no way you could be sure of your judgment. The Church greatly needs an intelligent system of clergy placement.

The fact that we do as well as we do now, with the blind leading the blind, must certainly indicate (a) that our clergy, by and large, are competent, consecrated men, and (b) that the holy Spirit does, in spite of the roadblocks we set up, somehow manage to help us.

Dissolving the Pastoral Relationship: This would not be a realistic manual if it failed to say something about the unhappy problem of how to break the relationship between Rector and parish. Most people do not put it quite so delicately. The usual expression is "getting rid of the Rector."

There are far too many situations in which a vacant parish, ignoring the advice of the Bishop, goes ahead and calls a clergyman who is singularly ill-fitted for that particular parish. (This is nothing against the clergyman. All it means is that his talents are not the necessary ones in this situation.)

Then, in a year or two, when it has become obvious that the Bishop was right in the first place, the parish appeals to him to move the man somewhere else. Even a Bishop would have a right to gloat a little in such a case, but it is too serious a matter for such indulgence.

A quick answer to the parish that wants to get rid of its Rector is "You can't." The relationship between Rector and parish is more like a marriage than a contract. They take each other for better or for worse. You can't get a divorce just on the ground that you did not use good judgment in selecting a spouse. In the case of Rector and parish you can't even get one on that old catch-all ground of "incompatibility."

Having said that, we can go on to point out that if you do have real grounds for wanting the relationship broken, there is a Canon that tells you how to go about it. The Canon says you must petition the Bishop, in writing. The Bishop may make the decision himself, or may take advice from his Standing Committee. In either case, the Bishop's answer is final. There is no appeal beyond him.

See Canon 45, Section 2, on pages 77-78.

13 SOME NOTES ON THE CANONS

CANON 13

Of Parish Vestries

Sec. 1. In every Parish of this Church the number, mode of election, and term of office of Wardens and Vestrymen, with the qualifications of voters, shall be such as the State or Diocesan law may permit or require, and the Wardens and Vestrymen elected under such law shall hold office until their successors are elected and have qualified.

Sec. 2. Except as provided by the law of the State or of the Diocese, the Vestry shall be agents and legal representatives of the Parish in all matters concerning its corporate property and the relations of the Parish to its Clergy.

Sec. 3. Unless it conflict with the law as aforesaid, the Rector, when present, shall preside in all the meetings of the Vestry.

That's all the national Canons say about Vestries. Your diocesan Canons will fill in the details about eligibility, mode of election, etc.

Nothing special is said about Wardens in this book because not much is said about them in the Canons. Your diocese may be more definitive, but national Canons mention Wardens only twice: in Canon 44, Sec. 4 (b), which includes them in the list of persons who may certify to the "Ecclesiastical Authority of the Diocese" that a local clergyman is not performing his duties; and in Canon 46, Sec. 1, which says that "the Churchwardens or other proper officers" shall let the Bishop know when the parish becomes vacant.

CANON 44

Of Ministers and Their Duties

Sec. 1 (a). The control of the worship and the spiritual jurisdiction of the Parish, are vested in the Rector, subject to the Rubrics of the Book of Common Prayer, the Canons of the Church, and the godly counsel of the Bishop. All other Ministers of the Parish, by whatever name they may be designated, are to be regarded as under the authority of the Rector.

(b). For the purposes of his office and for the full and free discharge of all functions and duties pertaining thereto, the Rector shall, at all times, be entitled to the use and control of the Church and Parish buildings with the appurtenances and furniture thereof.

(c). In a Missionary Cure the control and responsibility belong to the Priest who has been duly appointed to the charge thereof, subject to the authority of the Bishop.

. . . .

Sec. 2 (e). The Alms and Contributions, not otherwise specifically designated, at the Administration of the Holy Communion on one Sunday in each calendar month, and other offerings for the poor, shall be deposited with the Minister of the Parish or with such Church officer as shall be appointed by him, to be applied by the Minister, or under his superintendence, to such pious and charitable uses as shall by him be thought fit. During a vacancy the Vestry shall appoint a responsible person to serve as Almoner.

. . . .

Sec. 3 (a). It shall be the duty of every Minister of the Church to record in the Parish Register all Baptisms, Confirmations, Marriages, Burials, and the names of all Communicants within his Cure.

Observe that Canon 44 puts in the hands of the Rector full authority (and therefore full responsibility) for everything but money and property. It does imply, however, that he may delegate parts of his ministry to "other Ministers of the Parish," and although it undoubtedly means ordained ministers, it does not specifically say so. Thus it is possible without breaking the law to allow the laity their part in the Church's true function. Call this a loophole if you wish. It would be more accurate to call it a clause that was written before the layman's role in the Church was rediscovered and which, therefore, could not be either for or against the layman's ministry.

In regard to Section 2 (e), it seems necessary to say that there are parishes where this Canon is utterly ignored. Vestries can justify quite logically their seizure of this money for budgetary purposes; but can they justify the flagrant violation of a Canon? On the other, happier, side there is a growing trend toward designating the alms at all Holy Communion services, not just one a month, to the Rector's discretionary fund.

Section 3 (a) says nothing about any Vestry responsibility in the maintenance of the parish register, but there are many places where some individual Vestryman does help with it. There is much detailed deskwork in keeping this register up-to date, particularly the communicant list. It is often more than a busy, harassed Rector can keep up with.

CANON 6

Of Business Methods in Church Affairs

Sec. 1. In every Diocese, Missionary District, Parish, Mission and Institution, connected with this Church, the following standard business methods shall be observed:

(1). Trust and permanent funds and all securities of whatsoever kind shall be deposited with a Federal or State Bank, or a Diocesan Corporation, or with some other agency approved in writing by the Finance Committee or the Department of Finance of the Diocese or Missionary District, under either a deed of trust or an agency agreement, providing for at least two signatures on any order of withdrawal of such funds or securities.

But this paragraph shall not apply to funds and securities refused by the depositories named as being too small for acceptance. Such small funds and securities shall be under the care of the persons or corporations properly responsible for them.

(2). Records shall be made and kept of all trust and permanent funds showing at least the following:

(a) Source and date.
(b) Terms governing the use of principal and income.
(c) To whom and how often reports of condition are to be made.
(d) How the funds are invested.

(3). Treasurers and custodians, other than banking institutions, shall be adequately bonded; except treasurers of funds that do not exceed five hundred dollars at any one time during the fiscal year.

(4). Books of account shall be so kept as to provide the basis for satisfactory accounting.

(5). All accounts shall be audited annually by a Certified or Independent Public Accountant, or by such an accounting agency as shall be permitted by the Finance Committee or Department of Finance of the Diocese or Missionary District.

A certificate of audit shall be forwarded to the Bishop or Ecclesiastical Authority not later than July 1 of each year, covering the financial reports of the previous calendar year.

(6). All buildings and their contents shall be kept adequately insured.

(7). The Finance Committee or Department of Finance of the Diocese or Missionary District may require copies of any or all accounts described in this Section to be filed with it and shall report annually to the Convention of the Diocese, or Convocation of the Missionary District upon its administration of this Canon.

(8). The fiscal year shall begin January 1.

Sec. 2. The several Dioceses and Missionary Districts shall give effect to the foregoing standard business methods by the enactment of Canons appropriate thereto, which Canons shall invariably provide for a Finance Committee or a Department of Finance of the Diocese or Missionary District.

Sec. 3. No Vestry, Trustee, or other body, authorized by Civil or Canon law to hold, manage or administer real property for any Parish, Mission, Congregation, or Institution, shall encumber or alienate the same or any part thereof (save for the refinancing of an existing loan) without the written consent of the Bishop and Standing Committee of the Diocese, or the Bishop and Council of Advice of the Missionary District, of which the Parish, Mission, Congregation, or Institution is a part, except under such regulations as may be prescribed by Canon of the Diocese or Missionary District.

Canon 6 really spells it out for you. It may appear terribly detailed and demanding, but everything in it is there for the good of your parish and over the years experience has shown it to be feasible. Study the Canon carefully. Every Vestryman, not only the Treasurer, should know it thoroughly.

CANON 46

Of the Filling of Vacant Cures

Sec. 1. When a Parish or Congregation becomes vacant the Churchwardens or other proper officers shall notify the fact to the Bishop. If the authorities of the Parish shall for thirty days have failed to make provision for the services, it shall be the duty of the Bishop to take such measures as he may deem expedient for the temporary maintenance of Divine services therein.

Sec. 2. No election of a Rector shall be had until the name of the Clergyman whom it is proposed to elect has been made known to the Bishop, if there be one, and sufficient time, not exceeding thirty days, has been given to him to communicate with the Vestry thereon, nor until such communication, if made within that period, has been considered by the Parish or Vestry at a meeting duly called and held for that purpose.

Sec. 3. Written notice of the election, signed by the Church-wardens, shall be sent to the Ecclesiastical Authority of the Diocese. If the Ecclesiastical Authority be satisfied that the person so chosen is a duly qualified Minister, and that he has accepted the office, the notice shall be sent to the Secretary of the Convention, who shall record it. And such record shall be sufficient evidence of the relation between the Minister and the Parish.

Sec. 4. A Minister is settled, for all purposes here or elsewhere mentioned in these Canons, who has been engaged permanently, or for any term not less than one year, by any Parish, according to the rules of the Diocese in which such Parish is located.

Sec. 5. In case of the election of an Assistant Minister the name of the clergyman whom it is proposed to elect, shall be made known to the Bishop and sufficient time, not exceeding thirty days, shall be given him to communicate with the Rector and Vestry thereon.

Canon 46 needs no comment. It is included in support of Chapter 12.

CANON 45

Of the Dissolution of the Pastoral Relation

Sec. 2. If for any reason a Rector or Minister as aforesaid, or the body authorized to elect a Rector in the Parish committed to his charge, shall desire a separation and dissolution of the pastoral relation, and the parties be not agreed respecting a separation and dissolution, notice in writing may be given by either party to the Ecclesiastical Authority of the Diocese or Missionary District. The Bishop, in case the difference be not settled by his godly judgment, shall ask the advice and consent of the Standing Committee of the Diocese or of the Council of Advice of the Missionary District, and, proceeding with its aid and counsel, shall be the ultimate arbiter and judge. If the Diocese or Missionary District be vacant, the Ecclesiastical Authority shall select a Bishop of an adjacent Diocese or Missionary District to act as the Bishop, and with like force and effect. The judgment shall be either that the pastoral relation between the parties shall cease and determine at a time and upon terms therein specified, or that the said relation shall not be terminated; and such judgment shall be binding upon both parties. In the event of the failure or refusal of either party to comply with the terms of such judgment, the Bishop may inflict such penalties as may be provided by the Constitution and Canons of the Diocese or Missionary District; and in default of any provisions for such penalties therein, the Bishop may (1) in the case of a Rector or Minister, suspend such Rector or Minister from the exercise of his priestly office until he shall comply with said judgment; (2) in the case of a Vestry or Trustees, recommend to Diocesan Convention or Missionary Convocation and the union of the Parish or Mission with Convention or Convocation shall cease until they have complied with his judgment.

Extracanonical Notes: The "rotating Vestry" has become a popular institution. A rotating Vestry is one whose members are elected in classes, each class serving for a specified number of years (usually three) and then becoming ineligible for one year. For example, if you have twelve persons on your Vestry, you elect only four each year. These four serve for three years and at the end of their term cannot be re-elected until an interval of one year has passed.

This custom has assets that cannot be denied. It assures an infusion of new blood every year. Over the years it cannot fail to enlarge the number of people who are, or have been, on the Vestry. And, let's say it right out, it solves the problem of how to get rid of dead wood without embarrassment.

As far as I know, no one has questioned the legality of the

rotating Vestry, which every year rules ineligible several people whom the Canon declares to be eligible. Some dioceses have changed their Canon to provide for rotation. Others just go ahead and rotate even though their Canon would seem to prohibit it.

The time at which a Vestry meeting is held can sometimes be a very important consideration. You can rule certain people right off the Vestry by holding your meetings at times when they could not be present. For example a luncheon meeting, which is traditional in some parishes, could be impossible for a laboring man or many a mother with small children. Think about this when setting the time for your Vestry meetings.

Some parishes have found it a good idea to "rotate" the agenda at their meetings. For example, if you start this month's meeting with Treasurer's report and go on through the reports of the various committees, move the Treasurer to the bottom of the list next month, and follow the same rotating procedure each month. Over the course of a year this will guarantee that the same people do not get a quick, inadequate hearing every time.

APPENDIX

GLOSSARY OF USEFUL TERMS

Some words and expressions you'll want to know.

Acolyte: The boy who serves the priest at the altar at the Holy Communion service. Note—it does not have to be a boy; it can be a man. And he does not have to wear vestments. It is perfectly proper for any trained man or boy to go from his pew to the altar in his street clothes and serve the priest if no acolyte is on duty.

Alms: Nowadays this has come to mean the "loose offering," that is, the part of the offering that is not in pledge envelopes, at a service of Holy Communion.

Anglican Church: The world-wide totality of those national churches that are in communion with the Church of England and with one another.

Apocrypha: Fourteen books of the Bible that are not included by Anglicans in either the Old or New Testament but are put into an extra section between the two. The Church does not consider that they contain any material from which doctrine is established, but keeps them because of their value "for example of life and instruction of manners."

Archbishop: A Bishop who is in charge of a province (a group of dioceses) or who is the chief Bishop of some national branch of the Anglican Church. This does not apply, however, to our American Church; here the chief Bishop of the country is called the Presiding Bishop.

If you write a letter to an Archbishop, you address it to:

The Most Reverend ——— ———,

The Archbishop of ———

Speaking to him in person, you call him "Your Grace."

Archdeacon: A priest who, under the Bishop, has charge of the missionary work of the diocese or a part thereof. Call him Archdeacon when you speak to him, but when you write to him address the letter to The Ven. ——— ———. "Ven." stands for Venerable.

Bishop: Literally, "overseer." A clergyman of the highest of the three orders of the Christian ministry. Most Bishops, but by no means all, preside over dioceses. In America when we speak to

a Bishop we call him Bishop. Writing to him we write "The
Right Rev. ⸺ ⸺."

Canon: This word has a variety of meanings, of which two are
the most frequently used:

(1) Church law. The Canons are the rules and regulations of the
Church, enacted for the whole American Episcopal Church
by the General Convention. Further Canons, having special
reference to details of diocesan life, are enacted by the several
diocesan conventions.

Canons are mostly related to disciplinary matters rather than
to doctrine.

(2) An officer of a cathedral staff, usually a clergyman, though
there have been lay Canons. There are also honorary Canons,
appointed by the Bishop as honorary members of the cathedral staff. In either case, write to a Canon as The Rev. Canon
⸺ ⸺, and address him in direct conversation as
Canon ⸺.

Cathedral: The Bishop's church, the church where the Bishop's
"cathedra" (throne) is.

Celebrant: A priest who is officiating at a service of the Holy
Communion.

Chancel: The part of the church in which the choir stalls are
usually placed. Whether the choir is here or not, the chancel is
the area between the sanctuary and the nave.

Church Year: The nine seasons into which the year is divided by
the Church. They are: Advent, Christmas, Epiphany, Pre-Lent,
Lent, Easter, Ascensiontide, Whitsuntide, and Trinity. See
Hymn 235 for a good concise explanation of the meanings of
these seasons.

Coadjutor: An assistant bishop who is guaranteed the right of succession when the incumbent retires or dies.

Communicant: The American church has never yet agreed on just
what a communicant is. For a working definition, better just say
"a baptized, confirmed member in good standing."

Crucifer: The boy who carries the cross ahead of the choir in
procession. He is usually dressed in priestly vestments (amice
and alb), even in parishes where there would be a horrible to-do
if the priest himself wore them. It is also customary for him to
hold his arms in as awkward a position as he can manage and
still carry anything.

Curate: A clergyman who assists the Rector.

Deacon: A clergyman of the lowest of the three orders of the Christian ministry. He is usually a young man, probably just out of seminary, and will be a deacon only six months to a year before being advanced to the priesthood. There are, however, a few "perpetual" deacons.

Dean: The head of a cathedral, a seminary, or a rural deanery. The rural deans came first. Bishops divided the diocese into groups of ten parishes (decenaries—the word soon elided into deaneries) and appointed a clergyman at the head of each group. When this principle of government by tens passed into the college structure, seminaries began to have deans. Last of all, the head priest of a cathedral, as chief of about ten, came to be called a dean.

In all cases, write to or about a dean as The Very Rev. ——— ———. Call him "Dean ———."

Degrees: The letters you see behind the name of your Rector and other dignitaries. In Church usage, those most frequently seen are:

B.D.—Bachelor of Divinity. Most clergyman have this one if they have been graduated after a full three-year course in a seminary.

S.T.M.—Master of Sacred Theology. To get this one he put in an extra year at a seminary.

D.D.—Doctor of Divinity. An honorary degree given by a seminary to some of its alumni, and to particularly distinguished alumni of other institutions. It tells you nothing about the man's scholarly attainments, but it does tell you that the seminary (sometimes the man himself wonders why) has considered him worthy of this mark of esteem.

S.T.D.—Doctor of Sacred Theology. Sometimes honorary, but usually achieved the hard way—by three years of extra study after seminary.

Ph.D.—Doctor of Philosophy. This is not an ecclesiastical degree, but it is held by enough clergyman to justify including it here. This is always an earned degree. The man who holds it is a true scholar. You may be sure he knows a great deal about something.

Diocese: A geographical division of the Church, under the jurisdiction of a Bishop.

Episcopal: Literally, "of bishops." We are an Episcopal Church because we have Bishops. The Roman, Orthodox, and some other churches are episcopal, too.

Eucharist: Literally, " thanksgiving." Another name for the Holy Communion service. Still other names for this service are the Lord's Supper and the Mass.

Excommunication: Exclusion of a person from the sacramental life of the parish.

Executive Council: The "vestry" of the diocese. Persons elected by the diocesan convention to assist the Bishop in the adminis-tration of the diocese.

Font: The bowl that holds the water for Baptism.

General Convention: The legislative assembly of the American Episcopal Church, held every three years. It consists of two sections or houses: the House of Bishops, composed of all Bishops, and the House of Deputies, made up of clergy and laity. Each diocese sends four clergymen and four laymen; each mis-sionary district one clergyman and one layman.

Godparents: The adults who represent the child at Baptism by taking his vows for him and who promise to be responsible for his Christian education. The normal number of godparents is three, two of the same sex as the child and one of the opposite.

Holy Orders: The ranks or orders of the ordained ministry. Bishops, priests, and deacons are said to be "in" Holy Orders.

Lay reader: A layman who is licensed to lead public services of worship, with the exception of those services or parts of serv-ices that require a priest.

Lectern: The stand on which the Bible is placed in the church.

Narthex: That part of the church building that most people mis-takenly call the vestibule.

Nave: The part of the church where the people sit. It extends from the narthex to the chancel.

Parish Register: The book in which all communicants of the parish are listed and all Baptisms, confirmations, marriages, and burials are recorded. This very important document is required by Canon 45, Sec. 3 (a).

Postulant: A man who wishes to become a candidate for holy orders. Becoming a postulant is the first step in the process.

Rector: A priest who is in charge of a parish.

Rectory: The residence provided by the parish for the Rector.

Sacraments: The Church's definition is on page 292 of the Book of Common Prayer. The two sacraments are Baptism and Holy Communion. There are five other ordinances that many people call sacraments: confirmation, penance, orders, matrimony, and unction of the sick. The latter five are considered voluntary, for particular occasions or states of life.

Sanctuary: The part of the church building in which the altar stands.

Server: See *Acolyte.*

Sexton: The man everybody calls the janitor.

Sponsor: See *Godparents.*

Standing Committee: A permanent committee in every diocese which becomes the ecclesiastical authority in the diocese during periods in which there is no bishop. The standing committee consists of both clergy and laity elected by the diocesan convention. In normal times its duties are to pass on such legal matters as the sale of church property.

Suffragan: An assistant Bishop who does not have the right of succession to the Bishop's office.

Vicar: Literally, "substitute." A clergyman who has charge of a mission. If the mission is supported by a parish, the Vicar represents the Rector. If it is a diocesan mission, he is the Bishop's representative.

THE ADMISSION OF WARDENS AND VESTRYMEN

(Adapted from *The Book of Offices*)

¶ *To be used before the Liturgy, or after the Third Collect of Morning or Evening Prayer, or separately.*

¶ *A Sponsor shall be named (either a continuing member of the Vestry, or the Clerk of the Parish Meeting), who shall present the Candidates for Admission to Office.*

THE PRESENTATION

¶ *The Congregation being seated, the Priest shall stand at the Chancel Gate, facing the People, the Sponsor and the Candidates standing before him. The Sponsor shall say,*

REVEREND Sir, I present unto you these persons to be admitted as Wardens and Vestrymen in this Parish.

Priest. Are the persons whom you present duly elected, and prepared, by purity of life, regular attendance at Church, and knowledge of their duties, to exercise this ministry to the honour of God and the edifying of the Church?

Sponsor. I do certify their election and do believe them apt to this ministry.

THE EXAMINATION

¶ *The Priest, addressing the Candidates, shall say,*

DEARLY beloved, who desire to be admitted as Wardens and Vestrymen in this Parish, are you convinced that the work of this ministry is so important that, during the term of office for which you have been chosen, you should be diligent in performing the same?

Answer. I am so convinced.

Priest. Will you try faithfully and reverently to execute the duties of your Office to the best of your ability, as unto the Lord and not unto men, seeking, by earnest prayer, God's help thereto?

Answer. I will try so to do.

Priest. Will you strive to live in accordance with the sacredness of this Office?

Answer. I will so strive, the Lord being my helper.

Priest. May God guide and bless you in the doing of this work.

¶ *Then, all standing, the following Antiphon and Psalm shall be sung or said.*

Antiphon. Praise the Lord, ye servants; *O Praise the Name of the Lord.

Psalm 100. *Jubilate Deo*

O BE joyful in the Lord, all ye lands; *serve the Lord with gladness, and come before his presence with a song.

Be ye sure that the Lord he is God; it is he that hath made us, and not we ourselves; *we are his people, and the sheep of his pasture.

O go your way into his gates with thanksgiving, and into his courts with praise; *be thankful unto him, and speak good of his Name.

For the Lord is gracious, his mercy is everlasting; *and his truth endureth from generation to generation.

Glory be to the Father, and to the Son, *and to the Holy Ghost;

As it was in the beginning, is now, and ever shall be, *world without end. Amen.

THE ADMISSION

¶ *Then, the People being seated, one appointed shall read the following Lesson.*

The Lesson. Numbers 11:16

THE Lord said unto Moses, Gather unto me seventy men of the elders of Israel, whom thou knowest to be elders of the people, and officers over them; and bring them unto the tabernacle of the congregation, that they may stand there with thee. And I will come down and talk with thee there: and I will take of the spirit which is upon thee, and will put it upon them; and they shall bear the burden of the people with thee, that thou bear it not thyself alone.

¶ *Then shall the Priest proceed to admit the Candidates to their Office, taking each one by the right hand, and saying to each one, severally.*

The Admission

N., I ADMIT you to the Office of *Warden* (or, *Vestryman*) in this Parish; [and I give you this ———— as a Token of your Ministry][1] In the Name of the Father, and of the Son, and of the Holy Ghost. Amen.

¶ *When all have been admitted, the Priest shall continue as followeth.*

Antiphon. Without counsel purposes are disappointed: *but in the multitude of the counsellors they are established.
I am thy servant, O grant me understanding;
That I may know thy testimonies.

---

[1] The words within brackets are read where the custom is to present a Book of Canons or a cross to the inductee.

Let us pray.

O Eternal God, the fountain of all wisdom: Enlighten with thy grace the Wardens and Vestrymen of thy Church, and so rule their minds, and guide their counsels, that in all things they may seek thy glory and the welfare of thy holy Church; through Jesus Christ our Lord. *Amen.*

THE CONCLUSION

¶ *Here, if this Office has been used separately, may follow a Sermon or Instruction; and, this being ended, there shall follow the Three-fold Kyrie and the Lord's Prayer.*

¶ *Then shall the Priest say,*

Teach me thy way, O Lord, and I will walk in thy truth;
O knit my heart unto thee, that I may fear thy Name.
So will I always sing praise unto thy Name;
That I may daily perform my vows.
The Lord be with you;
And with thy spirit.

Let us pray.

Regard, we beseech thee, O Lord, our supplications, and confirm with thy heavenly benediction thy servants whom we have admitted to office and ministry of thy Church, that with sincere devotion of mind and body they may offer a service acceptable to thy divine Majesty; through Jesus Christ our Lord, to whom, with thee and the Holy Ghost, be all honour and glory, world without end. *Amen.*

¶ *Here, the Priest shall let them depart with a blessing, as followeth.*

GOD, the Alpha and Omega, who worketh in you both to will
and to do of his good pleasure, be himself the beginning and
the end of your work; and may the power of the Father, the
wisdom of the Son, the love of the Holy Spirit, the grace of
the blessed and undivided Trinity, be with you and preserve
you, now, henceforth, and for evermore. *Amen.*

OFFICE FOR A VESTRY MEETING

¶ The Vestry being assembled in the Chancel or in the Vestry Room, the Leader shall begin the Office as followeth, all standing.

IN the Name of the Father, and of the Son, and of the Holy Ghost. *Amen.*

I will declare thy Name unto my brethren;

In the midst of the congregation will I praise thee.

Glory be to the Father, and to the Son, and to the Holy Ghost.

As it was in the beginning, is now, and ever shall be, world without end. Amen.

Prosper thou the work of our hands upon us.

Deus misereatur. Psalm 67

God be merciful unto us and bless us, *and show us the light of his countenance, and be merciful unto us;

*That thy way may be known upon earth, *thy saving health among all nations.*

Let the peoples praise thee, O God; *yea, let all the peoples praise thee.

*O let the nations rejoice and be glad; *for thou shalt judge the folk righteously, and govern the nations upon earth.*

Let the peoples praise thee, O God; *yea, let all the peoples praise thee.

Then shall the earth bring forth her increase; and God, even our own God, shall give us his blessing.

God shall bless us; *and all the ends of the world shall fear him.

Glory be to the Father, and to the Son, *and to the Holy Ghost.

*As it was in the beginning, is now, and ever shall be, *world without end. Amen.*

All. Prosper thou the work of our hands upon us; *O prosper thou our handy work.

¶ *Then shall the Leader read*

The Chapter. Ephesians 4:11-13
AND he gave some, apostles; and some, prophets; and some, evangelists; and some, pastors and teachers; for the perfecting of the saints, for the work of the ministry, for the edifying of the body of Christ: till we all come in the unity of the faith, and of the knowledge of the Son of God, unto a perfect man, unto the measure of the stature of the fulness of Christ.
Leader. But thou, O Lord, have mercy upon us.
Answer. Thanks be to God.
Leader. The Lord be with you.
Answer. And with thy spirit.

Let us pray.

Lord, have mercy upon us.
Christ, have mercy upon us.
Lord, have mercy upon us.

OUR Father, who art in heaven, Hallowed be thy Name. Thy kingdom come. Thy will be done, On earth as it is in heaven. Give us this day our daily bread. And forgive us our trespasses, As we forgive those who trespass against us. And lead us not into temptation, But deliver us from evil. Amen.
Leader. Show thy servants thy work.
Answer. And their children thy glory.
Leader. Let thy merciful kindness, O Lord, be upon us.
Answer. As we do put our trust in thee.
Leader. Not unto us, O Lord, not unto us;
Answer. But to thy Name give the praise.

Leader. Lord, hear our prayer;
Answer. And let our cry come unto thee.
Leader. The Lord be with you.
Answer. And with thy spirit.

Let us pray.

ALMIGHTY God, we humbly beseech thee to bless this Church and parish, and to further with thy continual help those who labour in it in thy fear and for thy glory; grant them lowliness of spirit, steadfastness of faith, perseverance in all good works, and bring them at last to thy heavenly kingdom; through Jesus Christ our Lord. *Amen.*

¶ *Or this*

ALMIGHTY God, giver of all gifts, grant to the members of this Vestry, wisdom to avoid false choices, courage to follow our Lord's teachings, vision to see thy true calling for this parish, and the grace humbly to acknowledge thy Church universal, through Jesus Christ our Lord.

¶ *Or this*

BLESSED Lord, who has called us to this office in thy Church, guide us, we beseech thee, in our deliberations, so that all our aims and purposes may be to the strengthening of the work in this parish and the support of the Church's mission throughout the world; through Jesus Christ our Lord.

¶ *Then shall the Leader say*

GOD be gracious unto us, and give us all a heart to serve him, and to do his will with a good courage and a willing mind. *Amen.*

INDEX

95